WHOLE HEARTED

JORDAN LEE DOOLEY

Paige Tate & Co.

Copyright © 2016 Jordan Lee

Published by Paige Tate & Co.
Paige Tate & Co. is an imprint of Blue Star Press
PO Box 8835, Bend, OR 97708
contact@paigetate.com
www.paigetate.com

ISBN: 9781963183504

Printed in China

THIS DEVOTIONAL BELONGS TO

Lia Barnhart

hello!

I am so glad that you are embarking on this 30-day journey
with me. Studying the Word is a wonderful adventure, but
I know starting can be intimidating! I pray that as we study
these Scriptures together, we let the creativity of God's hand
pour over our hearts as we join Him in creating. I encourage
you to be yourself. You don't have to be an artist. You may
believe that you don't have a creative bone in your body.
But if your heart is beating and your lungs are pumping,
I invite you to detach from the world and dive into the Word.
I've titled this devotional "Wholehearted" because that's
what I pray this opportunity will be for you: a wholehearted
connection, study, and engagement with the Word, creatively and personally. Be bold, color outside the lines, and be
present throughout this 30-day devotional.

I DARE YA!

Or do you not know that your body is a temple of the Holy Spirit within you, whom you have from God? You are not your own, for you were bought with a price. So glorify God in your body.

1 CORINTHIANS 6:19-20

day 1

...for you were bought with a price.

1 CORINTHIANS. 6:20

I do a lot of critiquing. I struggle with shame and I tend to spend long periods of time in front of the mirror, picking apart every imperfection I can zero in on. I see a beautiful person and instantly struggle with comparison, forgetting my own unique beauty. We live in a world that measures worth in terms of beauty products, sex appeal, likes, followers, pounds, and dollars. We obsess over fading and fleeting forms of worth and neglect the eternal truth: our worth, our bodies, and our lives have eternal value. Maybe you get stuck in the rut, too. Maybe you worry about your appearance, feel ashamed of pesky sin, or question your worth as you stand in front of the mirror or on the scale. But here's the good news:

Our eternal worth is in one thing and one thing alone: Jesus on the cross, which reminds us of the price that was paid to restore us to a beautiful union with the Father. Christ loves us so much that He sacrificed His body in our place, laid down His life to take on what we deserve, and gave His guts to bring our bodies into glory. We are invited to embrace our true worth every time we look to the cross. Jesus paid the price. He gave worth to our bodies with His own body. Instead of hating our bodies, let's choose to honor the gifts that they are today. Let's be who we are with all of our imperfections and flaws. And let's love it!

RESPONSE:

Write a thank you note to God which describes three things about your physical appearance for which you are grateful.

Thank You, Daddy God, for my strong legs; for my eyes which sparkle with Your Joy & Life; and thank You for my smile, which welcomes people, brings them joy, and makes others feel loved & happy.

Thank You for my curly hair too! It's fun to play with.

PRAYER:

Please help me to value my body the way You do. To nourish it, care for it, and give it what it needs. Help me not to compare my body to anyone else's, for it is Your unique masterpiece.

Help me to accept my body how You made it, and believe it is perfect, because You say so. ♡

Abide in me, and I in you. As the branch cannot bear fruit by itself, unless it abides in the vine, neither can you, unless you abide in me. I am the vine; you are the branches. Whoever abides in me and I in him, he it is that bears much fruit, for apart from me you can do nothing. If anyone does not abide in me he is thrown away like a branch and withers; and the branches are gathered, thrown into the fire, and burned.

JOHN 15:4-6

day 2

Abide in me...

JOHN 15:4

When I was in high school, I used to cram a ton of information about art history or pre-calculus into my little brain just to regurgitate the information on a test, hoping for an A. As an adult, I notice that sometimes I try to put this practice into play when it comes to Kingdom work, too. And it's disastrous because I'm trying to produce fruit through efforts that stem from self-righteousness.

Unlike earning an A on a test, producing real spiritual fruit is something I'm incapable of on my own. But sometimes I still try to force it, like a branch cut off from the apple tree, lying on the ground trying to produce its own apple. *Just try a little harder! The fruit has to be coming soon!* I tell myself. But it doesn't. No matter how hard I try to squeeze out the fruit, it never even buds. No one is fed. No one is nourished. And I'm left tired, frustrated, and discouraged.

LIVE FOR GOD! LIVE FOR GOD! I see this everywhere. It's a hot phrase in Christian circles nowadays. As if having Christian celebrities and running big conferences are the points of being Christian. There's this whole idea of being a warrior for God. It's a great concept, but it gets a little twisted sometimes.

If you're questioning your ability to make an impact for God, I invite you to stop for a moment. It's never been about our ability or our influence. It's about God. Instead of obsessing over living *for* God, what if we just live *because* of God (Donehey, 2010)? The problem with living for God is that it quickly becomes about our efforts, performance, and praise. Living because of God is about Him: it's all about the Vine, the Life-Giver, Fruit-Producer.

I invite you to connect. Open your heart. Dwell. Abide. Live in perpetual yes. He will move, sometimes through others more than you and sometimes through you more than others. But if we're remaining in Christ and living simply with a "because of Him" mentality, all that will matter is that He is moving.

I am
the vine
you are
the
branches

JOHN 15:5

Do not work for the food that perishes, but for the food that endures to eternal life, which the Son of Man will give to you. For on him God the Father has set his seal." Then they said to him, "What must we do, to be doing the works of God?" Jesus answered them, "This is the work of God, that you believe in him whom he has sent." So they said to him, "Then what sign do you do, that we may see and believe you? What work do you perform? Our fathers ate the manna in the wilderness; as it is written, 'He gave them bread from heaven to eat.'" Jesus then said to them, "Truly, truly, I say to you, it was not Moses who gave you the bread from heaven, but my Father gives you the true bread from heaven. For the bread of God is he who comes down from heaven and gives life to the world." They said to him, "Sir, give us this bread always." Jesus said to them, "I am the bread of life; whoever comes to me shall not hunger, and whoever believes in me shall never thirst.

JOHN 6:27-35

day 3

For the bread of God... gives life to the world.

JOHN 6:33

I spend a lot of time working for the food that spoils. This world sucks me in like a vacuum, feeding me the lie that every single item on my to-do list, even folding socks, holds some great value. And I begin to question my worth if I fall behind on projects, chores, and Facebook.

You know, the Lord is awfully creative. He often uses some silly frustration to wake me up in the middle of all my doing—some little thing that sends me into a wicked fit of emotions that wouldn't have happened if I hadn't been so stressed. When I gather myself, I feel ridiculous for letting the slow Wi-Fi speed bother me. And I'm reminded of a simple truth: I'm investing too much time in things that have no eternal value. Sometimes folding socks and doing dishes and creeping on old friends on Facebook can be good. Well, maybe not the last one. But our earthly duties are not necessarily bad. It's when they begin to consume us that they gain the power to spoil our souls and our attitudes. Jesus reminds us in this passage to work, honor, and obsess over those things that hold eternal value—for the food that doesn't spoil. It nourishes, revives, restores, and preserves. Look at your to-do list, examine where you spend your time. Are you eating more of the bread that spoils, or filling your head and heart with the bread that has eternal value?

You are an eternal being. Live like it, love it, and feed your soul the food it really craves.

RESPONSE:

In what ways do you work only for "the food that perishes"? What does it mean to you for Jesus to be the bread of life?

_____
_____
_____
_____
_____
_____
_____
_____
_____
_____
_____

PRAYER:

_____
_____
_____
_____
_____
_____
_____
_____
_____
_____
_____
_____
_____

There is therefore now no condemnation for those who are in Christ Jesus. For the law of the Spirit of life has set you free in Christ Jesus from the law of sin and death. For God has done what the law, weakened by the flesh, could not do. By sending his own Son in the likeness of sinful flesh and for sin, he condemned sin in the flesh, in order that the righteous requirement of the law might be fulfilled in us, who walk not according to the flesh but according to the Spirit.

ROMANS 8:1-4

day 4

For the law of the spirit of life has set you free
in Christ Jesus from the law of sin and death.

ROMANS 8:2

A few months ago, I took a day trip with my fiancé. As we chatted
about Jesus, work, and ministry, he asked why I had become so quiet.
I began to tear up, covering my face with my scarf. If I were a turtle,
it would have been my "retreating into my shell" moment. You may
be asking, "Why?"

Because as we talked openly about salvation and the Kingdom, I
looked down at my dirty hands and felt immensely unworthy of such
love, salvation, and work. I felt inadequate and small. Perhaps you
struggle with that, too. Maybe you look back at a history of sin and
look forward, wondering how you're going to be a Christian or feel
worthy enough. We've created a cookie-cutter list of requirements
for dressing the part, for being a "Christian." If we really look at the
Gospels, though, we can powerfully resist the temptation to become
a performance-based Christian. Jesus came to abolish our tendency
to do that! I want you to come back out of your shell. I want to challenge you to say "no" to the lies that scream that you'll never be good
enough. The truth is, following Jesus doesn't require you to be good
enough because He is! To those of you who wish to retreat into your
shells, struggling to do good or be good, you are invited to rest easy.
Becoming a Christian doesn't make us perfect; rather, it rests in the
fact that we don't have to save ourselves. We can place our hope,
joy, purpose, and salvation in Jesus. When we do, no performance
is required. There is condemnation no more. There is no shame.

there is no condemnation for those in Christ Jesus

ROMANS 8:1

While walking by the Sea of Galilee, he saw two brothers, Simon (who is called Peter) and Andrew his brother, casting a net into the sea, for they were fishermen. And he said to them, "Follow me, and I will make you fishers of men." Immediately they left their nets and followed him.

MATTHEW 4:18-20

day 5

Follow me, and I will make you fishers of men.

MATTHEW 4:19

I really like sports. I grew up watching football with my dad, played basketball and soccer throughout middle and high school, and I'm currently engaged to a football player. I'm not sure if my body could make it up and down the court like I used to, but I can still shoot a mean jump shot on a good day. Sports are my thing, and I can speak the language of points and blitzes. Perhaps you have something you connect with, too. Maybe you're a reader and can speak the language of literature. Or maybe you're a baker and can communicate in recipes and pastries.

In this passage, Jesus did something interesting. He spoke the language of Peter and Andrew. They were fishermen. He met them and related to them. He didn't say, "Follow me and I will make you great disciples." That probably would have confused them. So Jesus spoke their language. He requested that they follow Him so that he could make them "fishers of men." In other words, they would bring in people like they brought in fish. This was a concept they could understand.

Jesus invites you and me to do the same thing. If you're a sports person, Jesus invites you to follow and promises victory. If you're a book person, Jesus invites you to follow and reads you the best story. If you're into baking, He invites you to follow and teaches you the sweetest recipe in the book. So to those of you questioning whether this whole following Jesus thing is worth it, translate the idea into the language you speak and understand. He's willing to use us in His mission. The requirement is that we follow. It's worth victory, sweet treats, and better stories. It is always worth it.

RESPONSE:

What does following Jesus look like to you? List the gifts and skills you possess that God could use for His mission.

_____

_____

_____

_____

_____

_____

_____

_____

_____

_____

_____

_____

PRAYER:

_____

_____

_____

_____

_____

_____

_____

_____

_____

_____

_____

_____

O Lord, you have searched me and known me!
You know when I sit down and when I rise up;

  you discern my thoughts from afar.

You search out my path and my lying down

  and are acquainted with all my ways.

Even before a word is on my tongue,

  behold, O Lord, you know it altogether.

PSALM 139:1-4

day 6

O Lord, you have searched me and known me!

PSALM 139:1

The other day I found myself checking in on old friends from high school on Facebook. As I sat there, I realized that everyone looks slightly different, older, than I remember. I can see a lot about their lives in a few photos and statuses—I see the shell, but I really *don't* know them. I don't know much about their hearts, beliefs, hardships, and stories. I just see a basic profile with snapshots of moments. I got to thinking: what if God only saw us as a profile? I think that sometimes, we begin to fall into the mindset that God sees the makings of our profile like it's all He cares about. But His love reaches so far beyond what we display on our walls and profiles. He knows our hearts, the deepest, darkest corners of them, and the places we wouldn't dare put on Facebook or showcase to the world. He sees beyond the snapshots of moments and celebrations. And He loves us more than we could dream, regardless of what He finds. Don't fall into the trap of performance Christianity. You don't have to report your church attendance, inform anyone that you're doing well, or promote your works of charity for the year. Let the truth of His far-reaching love compel you forward today. The deepest parts of your being are fully known and fully loved!

CELEBRATE IT!

O Lord, you have searched me and known me

PSALM 139:1

...so that by two unchangeable things, in which it is impossible for God to lie, we who have fled for refuge might have strong encouragement to hold fast to the hope set before us. We have this as a sure and steadfast anchor of the soul, a hope that enters into the inner place behind the curtain...

HEBREWS 6:18-19

day 7

We have this as a sure and steadfast anchor of the soul...

HEBREWS 6:18-19

I noticed two big words in Barack Obama's 2008 campaign: HOPE and CHANGE. They struck me. In something as secular as politics, a deep longing of every human heart surfaced. We all speak the language of hope, Don't we? When it comes to change, we can all recognize things that aren't quite right in the world, things that we hope to change. Isn't that interesting? We all hope for something better, something more right, more harmonious. We see the hopelessness, corruption, and suffering of this world and hope for a change.

We need a change that only God can bring—hope that only Jesus can offer. So if you're in a season of pain, hardship, uncertainty, or deep suffering, let down any walls of protection that you've built around your heart. You don't need those defenses. Choose instead to reflect and receive the hope Jesus hands you on a big silver platter, sealed with His blood.

Change is on the way.

RESPONSE:

What walls in your life need to come down for you to fully lean into the hope
Jesus offers?

_____

_____

_____

_____

_____

_____

_____

_____

_____

_____

_____

PRAYER:

_____

_____

_____

_____

_____

_____

_____

_____

_____

_____

_____

_____

_____

...that according to the riches of his glory he may grant you to be strengthened with power through his Spirit in your inner be-ing, so that Christ may dwell in your hearts through faith—that you, being rooted and grounded in love, may have strength to comprehend with all the saints what is the breadth and length and height and depth...

EPHESIANS 3:16-18

day 8

...so that Christ may dwell in your hearts through faith

EPHESIANS 3:17

Some days I feel useless. I begin to ask questions like, "Does my life really matter?" "What is my purpose here?" "What is God's will for my life?" Maybe you do the same runaround. I think that often, we begin to believe that our purpose is in our work or accomplishments. But in this passage, Paul tells us something profound about our purpose. As followers of Jesus, we are rooted and established in His love so that we may have strength to understand the magnitude of His love and share it with others. But what do these terms mean when it comes to our identity and our purpose?

ROOTED: Refers to agriculture. Having roots in love makes it a life source. So not only are we created out of love, but the very roots of our existence are planted deep within its nutrient soil.

ESTABLISHED: Refers to structure. Love is the structure out of which our purpose, faith, and life are built. It is the cornerstone that supports all of our movements as believers. It is a sheltering structure to protect us, build us, and establish us in His ways.

We are planted in love: built by love, for love. Paul prays that we may grow in this understanding, because when we know how loved we truly are, we can act out of love. We can thus fulfill the greatest purpose of all: love God and love His people.

so that Christ may dwell in your hearts through faith

EPH 3:17

And Jesus said to his disciples,

"Truly, I say to you, only with difficulty will a rich person enter the kingdom of heaven. Again I tell you, it is easier for a camel to go through the eye of a needle than for a rich person to enter the kingdom of God." When the disciples heard this, they were greatly astonished, saying, "Who then can be saved?" But Jesus looked at them and said, "With man this is impossible, but with God all things are possible."

MATTHEW 19:23-26

day 9

...but with God all things are possible.

MATTHEW 19:26

Have you ever tried to carry something much heavier than you are physically able to lift? You know, when you're using all your might to move something that just won't budge? Me too. A few weeks ago, I tried to move a big box. I tried lifting, pushing, pulling, and kicking. But it was too heavy to move on my own. Anyone could have looked at my small frame next to the giant box and told me it would be impossible to move.

Thankfully, we're told in this passage that when life gets that heavy and things feel impossible, we don't have to rely on our own strength. Although Jesus is teaching about how difficult it can be for the rich to enter the kingdom of heaven, His closing words offer a sense of comfort in a seemingly discouraging story. He reminds His followers that although things may seem impossibly difficult, hope isn't lost. I've faced a lot of heavy boxes and struggled with a lot of shame in life. Many of those seasons seemed as if they were impossible to get through. So to those of you feeling the weight of the world, questioning how to get everything done, or wondering if you have the strength to make it through another day; there is sweet news for you. If God's power is enough to make a big, fat camel with two humps fit through the eye of a tiny needle, His power will get you through today. I promise you that.

RESPONSE:

How could you rely on God's strength instead of your own this week?

_____

_____

_____

_____

_____

_____

_____

_____

_____

_____

_____

_____

PRAYER:

_____

_____

_____

_____

_____

_____

_____

_____

_____

_____

_____

_____

_____

An excellent wife who can find?

She is far more precious than jewels.

PROVERBS 31:10

day 10

She is far more precious than jewels.

PROVERBS 31:10

This past year, I noticed something about what all of the Black Friday sales advertisements were really promising me. Beauty product ads promised to make me pretty enough. Clothing and shoe sales promised to make me stylish enough.

Gadget promotions promised to make me social and popular enough. Office supply sales promised to make me productive and successful enough. The list could go on and on.

All these advertisements suggest to me where I fall short and what I "need" in order to fix my shortcomings. Maybe you look out your window, at your phone, or into your TV and feel bombarded with these lies, too. If you're struggling to feel worthy, beautiful, or productive enough, I've got a little thing to tell you. You're already worth more than rubies, just as you are. Contrary to popular thought, we don't have to become or do enough. Why? Because enough has been done. Two thousand years ago, on a cross. And that makes you and me worth more than the most precious diamonds. You're a gem. And you're so worth it.

she is far more precious than jewels

PROV. 31:10

Do not be anxious about anything, but in everything by prayer and supplication with thanksgiving let your requests be made known to God. And the peace of God, which surpasses all understanding, will guard your hearts and your minds in Christ Jesus.

PHILIPPIANS 4:6-7

day 11

Do not be anxious about anything.

PHILIPPIANS 4:6

I admit it. I worry about some really silly things. I hide these silly worries deep in a pile of mental rubble, hoping that the Lord never sees them because I know that there are much bigger issues to worry about. People are starving and terror strikes across the globe—He certainly doesn't have time to hear about my little worries about the minor details of my life, right?

Wrong. If you're like me, you have some really big worries but also some seemingly insignificant ones that float around in the back of your mind. And if you're like me, you probably neglect to lay down all of your troubles before the Lord. This passage reminds us that God wants to take all of our burdens and all of our troubles. We don't need to be anxious in anything. Just as a parent wants to be there for their child in all things, our Father wants to be there for us in all things as well! Just like a parent cares about a child's grade on a math test and what Sally said at recess, He cares about the big stuff and the itty-bitty details. If you've been neglecting just to let it all spill out before Him, I challenge you to make a choice. Choose to be open, to approach Him with the big things and the little things. He promises to give peace in return.

Nothing, not one thing, is too small for God.

RESPONSE:

Set a timer for one minute and write out everything that makes you anxious. Set a timer for one minute and write out everything for which you are thankful. What requests do you need to bring to God?

_____

_____

_____

_____

_____

_____

_____

_____

_____

_____

_____

PRAYER:

_____

_____

_____

_____

_____

_____

_____

_____

_____

_____

_____

_____

_____

_____

He must increase, but I must decrease.

JOHN 3:30

day 12

He must increase, but I must decrease.

JOHN 3:30

Selflessness. It's a Christian buzzword that we hear a lot. Sometimes, it makes me cringe because I know how much it doesn't describe the true state of my heart. Perhaps you can relate. It sounds great and noble in theory, it's what we're called to. But practicing it can be so hard, right?

Selflessness is impossible without grace. Selflessness is impossible without Jesus. The truth here is that we do not need "more of Jesus." In reality, we already have all of Jesus. (How sweet is that?!) He is always fully and totally available. Jesus is always "all-there", serving us in love and mercy. What we need is less self.

Tim Keller, a pastor and author, puts it well: "We don't need to think less of ourselves, but to think of ourselves less (Keller, 2012)." Humility and selflessness are not putting myself down or depriving myself of enjoyment. Rather, it's choosing to make a larger space for Jesus and His people in our lives. It's minimizing not how we think of ourselves or serve ourselves, but how often we think of ourselves or serve ourselves. It's a greater concern for others and for Jesus. Jesus is already great, whether we let Him in or not. But today let's choose to expand the circle and make a greater space for Him in our lives. He deserves it.

He must increase
but I must decrease

JOHN 3:30

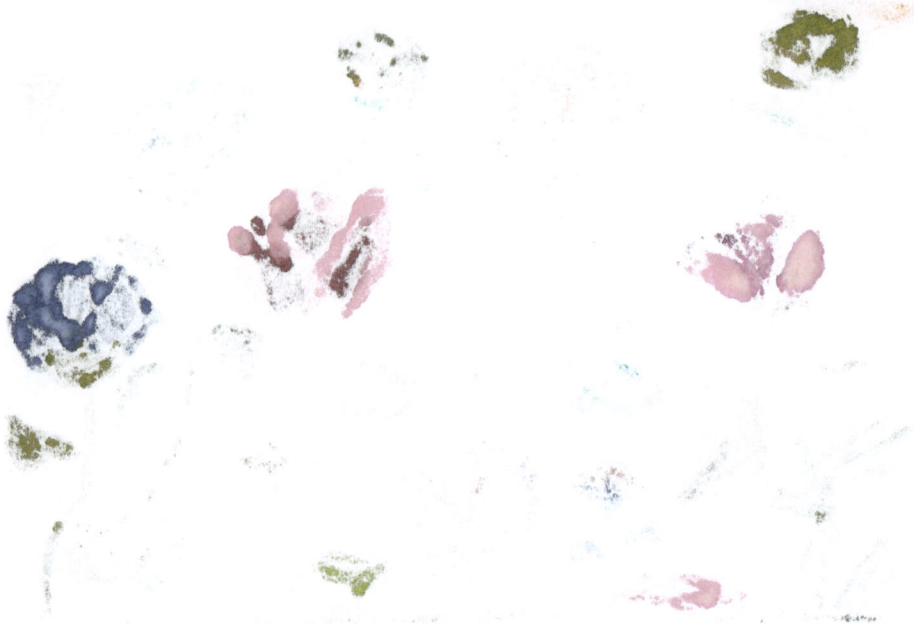

...Therefore, since we are surrounded by so great a cloud of witnesses, let us also lay aside every weight, and sin which clings so closely, and let us run with endurance the race that is set before us, looking to Jesus, the founder and perfecter of our faith, who for the joy that was set before him endured the cross, despising the shame, and is seated at the right hand of the throne of God...

HEBREWS 12:1-11

day 13

For the Lord disciplines the one he loves.

HEBREWS 12:6

A few years ago I slipped on my tennis shoes as I peered out the window of my living room. To my dismay, I saw a newly fallen frost. I was training for a half-marathon and it was a cold day in the Midwest. On top of that, the workout for the day was a hill workout. I almost slipped off my tennis shoes and crashed on the couch, but my running buddy called me and asked if I was ready. I told her I felt no motivation today, but she insisted I join her. As I ran up another hill in the frigid air, I was tired and angry that I had chosen to put myself through such torture. In my frustration and fatigue, I quickly lost sight of the reward that would come when I made it through the finish line on race day. After I finished the half-marathon, though, I realized how glad I was that I hadn't thrown in the towel when the going got tough. Discipline is work. It can be excruciatingly painful and hard and sometimes really cold. But here's the beauty of it: if we discipline ourselves for the sake of the greatest reward, we can be confident in the fruit that will come later on. Training for godliness and disciplining ourselves in the way of Christ helps us know our Creator more truly and intimately (Hughes, 2013). So if you find yourself growing weary, running low on hope and motivation, or facing a big hill, I want you to know that you have a running buddy—a friend. You're not alone in this training, this trial, or this life. Keep pressing on, keep running. The finish line is getting closer.

RESPONSE:

What practices can you do today to train in righteousness?

_____

_____

_____

_____

_____

_____

_____

_____

_____

_____

_____

_____

PRAYER:

_____

_____

_____

_____

_____

_____

_____

_____

_____

_____

_____

_____

Even when we were dead in our trespasses,
made us alive together with Christ—by grace
you have been saved.

EPHESIANS 2:5

day 14

...by grace you have been saved.

EPHESIANS 2:5

Not too long ago, I went to drop a package off at the post office. A jolly old man was sitting in a wheelchair there, and I walked past him toward the counter. I looked up to see him smiling as he bellowed, "Hello darlin', have a great day!"

You know, the skeptic in me would have been concerned at his forward friendliness. Our world nowadays tells us not to trust anyone and to ignore the lowly. But I paused. This was a simple yet divine appointment that God gave me to see His overflowing grace. The Lord cracked my shell, reminding me that good people, true joy, and humble hope still exist. And sometimes, they come in the form of a jolly man sitting in a wheelchair. Maybe in a society of individuality, productivity, and popularity, we need the humble hearts to crack through to our own and remind us of pure goodness and grace. In the middle of my running around, his warm greeting allowed me to see a thread of God's grace. Because this man truly had it figured out: he freely gave joy and grace away to the least expecting heart, to people like me. Friends, we are saved by grace! I am. You are. We all are.

So whether you feel like you're at rock bottom, or soaring with wings above the clouds, scatter grace like my friend at the post office. Regardless of the state of our conditions, let's choose not to forget what saves us. We are given the sweetest grace-cakes every morning so that we may freely give away grace-cakes to His people that surround our days. Let's do it together!

by grace
you have
been saved

EPH. 2:5

And I am sure of this, that he who began a good work in you will bring it to completion at the day of Jesus Christ.

PHILIPPIANS 1:6

day 15

... that he who began a good work in you will bring it to completion...

PHILIPPIANS 1:6

I love construction. I know, it sounds weird. But throw on a hard hat and dive into this one with me.

I do a lot of driving and a lot of running. I often pass by construction sites without giving them much thought. But as I sat at a stoplight across the street from a new house being built, something was written on my heart. That home in progress was a very accurate reflection of myself. It was dirt being turned up from the earth, shifted, mounded, and molded. It was a hole dug deep into the ground, creating space for growth. It was a cornerstone, laid down for stability. It was building upward, crafting the infrastructure that would support the roof. It was a process, a true process. I often think that the process stops when the building looks complete, when the goal is seemingly met, or the dream accomplished. But I forget that the owner of that house may have much grander plans and that it doesn't stop when the four walls and roof are in place. On the outside, it may look complete, but it's not. It's constantly evolving. On the inside, there's decorating to be done: furniture to change, walls to be painted, pictures to hang, and perhaps new additions will be added over time.

You see, what we consider complete is only part of the process. It's only a piece of the bigger plan. Even when we think we've become the person we want to be or achieved what we had hoped to achieve, it's truly so much bigger.

We are constantly being shaped, molded, built, and changed. We are under construction. But we have a repairman, a builder, a painter, a cornerstone, and a refuge in Christ Jesus. Whether you are feeling complete and perfect or damaged and in need of a fresh coat of paint, don't forget that this is part of the process. You are loved not for what you will be in the future but for what you are now. Whether you feel like a hole being dug into, heaps of clay being molded, or a roof being rebuilt, you are an incredibly valuable part of the process to the homeowner: the Father. Because He who began a good work in you will see to its completion.

RESPONSE:

What is God working on in your life right now? What work is in process?

_____
_____
_____
_____
_____
_____
_____
_____
_____
_____

PRAYER:

_____
_____
_____
_____
_____
_____
_____
_____
_____

Rejoice in the Lord always;
again I will say, rejoice.

PHILIPPIANS 4:4

day 16

Rejoice in the Lord always.

PHILIPPIANS 4:4

Sometimes I get really grumpy. I mean roll-your-windows-up-and-scream-till-you-cry grumpy. Life can be emotionally exhausting! Perhaps you've been feeling it recently. We may not always feel happy, but joy from Christ is not emotional. Which is good news, because my joy in Christ allows me to find joy in the ordinary. Joy can be found in the menial tasks: in diapers, punching a clock, exercise, relationships, work, play, and hardship. We can find joy in all things.

Invite Jesus into every area of your life by unconditionally rejoicing in His goodness. Seek Him in the places that bring feelings of resentment or irritation. Even in these places His blessings are there. He is working in the humblest and hardest of places, whether it's waiting at the doctor's office, folding endless loads of laundry, or mourning the loss of a loved one. When we adopt an eternal perspective, we will see His work far beyond the surface of our daily circumstances. Each of these not-so-glamorous and not-so-easy areas of our lives are places where He is present and active. Rejoice in these places, for His goodness always present.

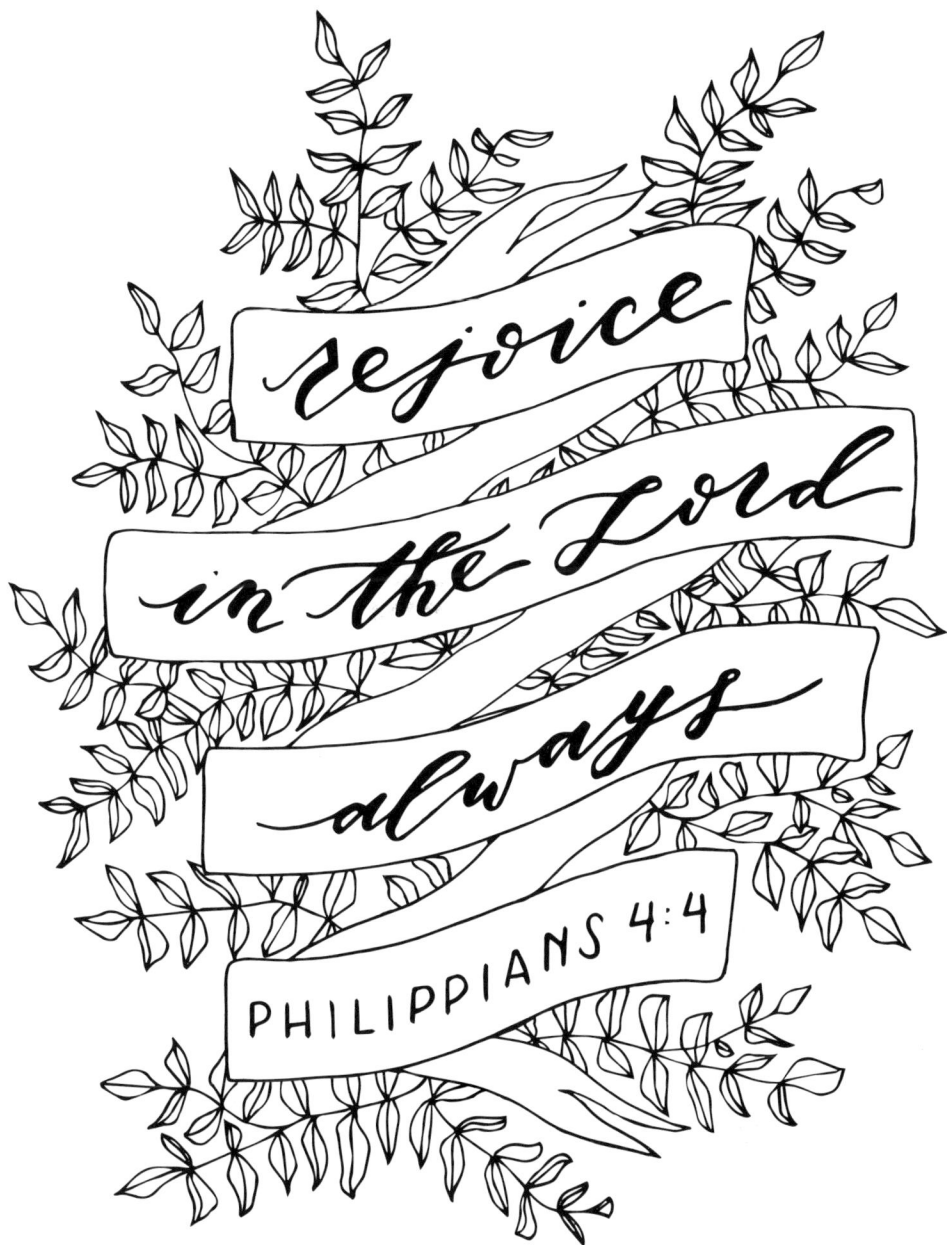

rejoice in the Lord always

PHILIPPIANS 4:4

After this the Lord appointed seventy-two others and sent them on ahead of him, two by two, into every town and place where he himself was about to go. And he said to them, "The harvest is plentiful, but the laborers are few. Therefore pray earnestly to the Lord of the harvest to send out laborers into his harvest. Go your way; behold, I am sending you out as lambs in the midst of wolves."

LUKE 10:1-3

day 17

The harvest is plentiful, but the laborers are few.

LUKE 10:2

I'm a worrywart. I worry about everything. I'm terrified to begin
something new because I fear my inability to follow through. I
become discouraged easily. Sometimes I get entangled in the ene-
my's lie that I'm not good enough, strong enough, eloquent enough,
or influential enough. There are a plethora of reasons to say no to
the work of the kingdom. But there's also one big reason to say yes:
Jesus is worth it. Every day we can look out our window, into the big
world around us. And every day we have a choice. We can look at the
opportunities that arise and let our doubts and feelings of inadequacy
keep us inside, feeling too small or incapable of making a difference.
Or, we can choose to be available and walk out the door. You see,
Jesus seeks the available, not the spectacular. The possibilities are
abundant, but walking out the door to take them is hard. It's simple,
but incredibly difficult. If you struggle with inadequacy and comparison, I want to remind you that you don't have to be spectacular, you
just need to be willing. Jesus was spectacular: He already saved the
world, and the pressure is off. He just asks us to go into His fields.
I challenge you to let go of comparison and walk out the door with
open hands. Because not only are the opportunities abundant, but
so is the supply and so are the possibilities when our lives are rooted
in the One, who is spectacular.

RESPONSE:

What is stopping you from going out into the fields and doing the work you believe God might be calling you to do?

_____

_____

_____

_____

_____

_____

_____

_____

_____

_____

_____

PRAYER:

_____

_____

_____

_____

_____

_____

_____

_____

_____

_____

_____

_____

_____

Iron sharpens iron, and one man sharpens another.

PROVERBS 27:17

day 18

...and one man sharpens another.

PROVERBS 27:17

Have you ever felt so spiritually dry that you began to question God's presence and existence in your life? I have, too. I remember one time in particular, during my freshman year of college. I had grown up in a Christian home, but when I was plopped down in a new town of over 50,000 students, far from my family, my bubble popped. And I kind of liked it. I was tired of only being around Christians all the time. I began to wonder if God really loved me as I developed "friendships" with anyone who was nice to me. After awhile, I found myself without a single friend who even asked about my faith. It wasn't a subject or a priority. As that year drew to a close, I felt empty and alone, so I decided to attend a church service. The preacher said something that has stuck with me for years and years: "Think of a wheel. A wheel is round and balanced so that it can rotate smoothly. We need a balanced amount of both stewardship and fellowship in our relationships so that we can sharpen others as well as be sharpened (Navigators)." I sat there with a whole new understanding. Growing up, my wheel was unbalanced with more fellowship than stewardship. But that year, my wheel was still unbalanced with more stewardship than fellowship.

Think about your wheel. Are you unbalanced? Remember to be intentional in seeking people who fill and sharpen you in Christ but don't forget to be willing to speak life into the lives of those who don't know Jesus. We can't have stewardship relationships without first developing fellowship with believers who strengthen us in Jesus. Nor can we stay comfortable in our fellowship bubbles without reaching out. I challenge you to evaluate your wheel, take note of who sharpens you, and how you sharpen others. It may just be a game-changer!

iron sharpens iron, and one man sharpens another

PROV. 27:17

You will seek me and find me, when you
seek me with all your heart.

JEREMIAH 29:13

day 19

...seek me with all your heart.

JEREMIAH 29:13

I just looked at my most recent Google searches. One that struck me was, "Should I get married in a church or outside?" I want to know God's will for the way in which I do things, but sometimes I find myself becoming so obsessed with finding an answer that I forget why I do things to begin with. As a result, in a desperate attempt to find an answer, I do a lot of web surfing. I ask Siri and Google far too many questions that I could find a better answer to in prayer. Perhaps you've found yourself doing this, too. And perhaps, after hours of surfing, you still fail to feel secure with a clear answer that really satisfies your heart. At least, that's the case for me. Why? Because the truth is, we are essentially looking for an answer that is not ours to know yet. Rather than insisting on finding the right answer, we can rest in the certainty of the One who is the answer— Jesus Himself (Stone, 2014). Seeking God wholeheartedly in our search for answers can draw us nearer to the heart of God and help us live in His will. Although we may not always fully understand Him, we can always fully trust Him. So if you're feeling lost or uncertain, take heart! You're not alone. Be encouraged in the truth that whenever we feel lost or unsure, He never loses us and He is always steady and sure. He is right there, unwavering.

RESPONSE:

How could you form a lifestyle that centers on seeking God?

_____

_____

_____

_____

_____

_____

_____

_____

_____

_____

_____

_____

PRAYER:

_____

_____

_____

_____

_____

_____

_____

_____

_____

_____

_____

_____

_____

For we walk by faith, not by sight.

2 CORINTHIANS 5:7

day 20

For we walk by faith, not by sight.

2 CORINTHIANS 5:7

There's an old saying: "seeing is believing." And you know, I often wish I had a telescope that allowed me to peer into the future, to see what it holds. And sometimes I'd like to add another feature to that telescope—one that allows me to see through the gates of heaven and look upon God's face. Surely, that would squash all the doubts that my heart wrestles with when life gets hard. But that would also squash the entire beauty of faith because faith argues the opposite of that old saying. Faith says, "believing is seeing." When we believe, and choose to walk in faith rather than by sight, we are living in the Spirit who bears faithfulness in us because we see and feel Him in our hearts rather than with our eyes. If you're struggling to remain faithful, let me remind you that His faithfulness remains when ours is shaky. Believe that truth and see it in your heart. And I'd be willing to bet that if you're anything like me, you can look back on your life and see all of the countless ways He has been faithful. So look forward, and believe that He is capable. Faith is the telescope that makes it possible to see into our hearts.

we walk by faith not by sight

2 COR. 5:7

For from his fullness we have all received,
grace upon grace.

JOHN 1:16

day 21

...grace upon grace.

JOHN 1:16

A few weeks ago, I went to Starbucks, ordered a latte, and stood there looking at the barista with an awkward, toothy grin as I realized I didn't have my wallet. Shoot. Thankfully, he let it slide. I was still able to enjoy a latte, although I wasn't able to pay for it.

Shortly after that happened, a friend of mine, Jake, shared an analogy he had recently heard using a very similar situation to describe God's grace. Here's what he shared: He used almost the exact situation—forgetting your wallet when going to the coffee shop—to describe the debt we are in to God. But he took it a step further, asking, "What if I forget my wallet again the next day? Would the barista give me grace again?" My friend went on, sharing that the barista might let it slide again but if the pattern continued, eventually Mr. Barista wouldn't be okay with it. And I'd be in debt to him.

And then, he shared something that really got me in the heart. What if I had a friend who knew how forgetful I was, went to my usual Starbucks, and gave the barista a card to charge my lattes to every time I forget my wallet? The next time I forgot to bring my wallet, I would stand there with an embarrassed grin again. But this time, the barista wouldn't have to let it slide. He would look at me and say, "It has already been paid for."

I put myself back in that situation, trying to imagine what that would be like. And I think I would stand in awe of a friend who would pay my debt over and over again, every time I forget to do it right. I thought it was a perfect example (especially for someone who loves coffee) so I just had to share it with you, too! I later learned that my friend originally heard the analogy from Pastor Mike Erre of VOX Community, who used it to explain how it's God's justice that gives us salvation from sin, not just His mercy.

When we surrender our lives to Jesus, lay down our righteousness, and trust Him as our Savior, the debt is paid in full and God pours something better than coffee into our cups. He pours grace upon grace.

Isn't that humbling to think about?

RESPONSE:

Describe a moment of grace in your life where someone did something unexpected for you? What image comes to mind when you hear the phrase "grace upon grace"?

_____
_____
_____
_____
_____
_____
_____

PRAYER:

_____
_____
_____
_____
_____
_____
_____

Create in me a clean heart, O God,
and renew a right spirit within me.

PSALM 51:10

day 22

...renew a right spirit within me.

PSALM 51:10

A pure heart? A steadfast spirit? Please, I'm not qualified. It sounds like quite a lofty goal, wouldn't you say? Even in our own corners of the universe, our circles of influence or respective ministries and work, selfishness and pride are sneaky. They find little crevices to sneak into our hearts and overtake any purity that remains. And suddenly, our hearts don't look so pure and our spirits struggle to stand firm. But notice how this verse begins. It doesn't say, "I will make a pure heart and I will try harder to have a steadfast spirit." Instead, it starts off with the request to God that He create a pure heart and renew a steadfast spirit, recognizing the need for Him to make these things possible. The creation of a pure heart and steadfast spirit doesn't come from our efforts, and it's not a result of trying harder. The creation of a pure heart results only from a life in Christ. When we say yes to Jesus, submitting our hearts and spirits to Him, He alone can make all things pure in the eyes of the Father. Hold onto that hope if you're feeling stained with impurity and a little less than steadfast. He makes you new, pure, and firm.

create in me a clean heart

PSALM 51:10

So, whether you eat or drink, or whatever
you do, do all to the glory of God

1 CORINTHIANS 10:31

day 23

... do all to the glory of God.

1 CORINTHIANS 10:31

When I was a kid, I played driveway basketball with my brother. If one of us pulled too far ahead in the score or did something to gain an advantage, the other would instantly yell, "That doesn't count!" After bickering about it, we'd often agree to redo and forget whatever points or advantage "didn't count." Things that don't count are considered meaningless: they hold no weight, they don't affect the score or the outcome. They are stricken from the record and forgotten.

Do you ever feel like you don't count? Or like you should give up the game when you fall behind? Ever feel like what you contribute holds no weight or significance? I want to remind you that unlike children's games, everything you do matters as long as you do it because of God. Maybe you're in pain, losing to an opponent, and feeling as if your points don't count. The difference with God is that it all counts. He says that He just wants you. He doesn't need your work, or your ministry, or your points, He just wants your heart. Give Him your heart in all the big things and in all the little things, when you're winning the game and when you're losing. You are purposefully placed on this court by the greatest Coach of all time. Play on, sweet friend. For Him, for His team, and for His glory.

RESPONSE:

List reasons why God might have placed you in your current circumstances right now. What might God be working on through you today?

_____
_____
_____
_____
_____
_____
_____
_____
_____
_____
_____
_____

PRAYER:

_____
_____
_____
_____
_____
_____
_____
_____
_____
_____
_____
_____
_____

But godliness with contentment is great gain.

1 TIMOTHY 6:6

day 24

But godliness with contentment is great gain.

1 TIMOTHY 6:6

I have a friend who battles cerebral palsy. He often shares the deep frustrations that his daily life brings. And that's okay. It's good. I encourage it. It's okay to get angry sometimes. We're only human. But you know, through his struggles, he has developed such a compassionate heart. He hugs tighter and smiles bigger than anybody I know. And it strikes me every time because he reflects the heart of one whose joy is not defined by circumstances.

So to those of you waking up to financial frustrations, emotional turmoil, or physical pain every day, this is for you: it's okay to get frustrated. It's okay to cry. It's okay to roll your windows up and scream really loud. But don't stop believing in good. Choose to hug tighter and smile bigger; keep waking up and facing the world every day, because this life and this pain are temporary. Although it may really wear you down, don't forget what joy truly is: joy is the God-given satisfaction that our friend Jesus made us right with our God, once and for all. He's alive and active in our lives and offers us the hope that we don't have to be our own savior. We can be content in all circumstances and conditions. The rare jewel of Christian contentment will be yours when everything that God is and all that He has done in Jesus fills your heart (Hughes, 2013).

BUT

godliness

WITH

contentment

IS GREAT GAIN

1 TIM. 6:6

For I long to see you, that I may impart to you some spiritual gift to strengthen you— that is, that we may be mutually encouraged by each other's faith, both yours and mine."

ROMANS 1:11-12

day 25

...that we may be mutually encouraged by each other's faith.

ROMANS 1:12

The other day, I was out running errands when I noticed a woman on the side of the road. She wasn't asking for anything. She was just standing there, waiting. I had a strong urge to turn around. I pulled up next to her. When I asked if she needed a ride, her eyes lit up as she nodded that she did.

As we drove, she told me her story. "I recently moved back to the area, but I'm living with my aunt. At my age, it's so hard to start over. I have no car. I have no place of my own. No job. Nothing. But I've been down and out before, and God worked it out for me. I keep praying to Jesus that He will again. You stopping to help me is proof that He hasn't forgotten me."

She also shared with me that she had walked over four miles to a bus stop and waited on a bus for over two hours so that she could go downtown and apply for jobs. But the bus never came, and she didn't have a phone to call the station. Businesses were going to close at 5 o'clock. It was 4 o'clock when I picked her up. Talk about just in time!

So to those of you in a rush, trying to do enough and be enough: don't forget to live an interruptible life. Look for opportunities to see heaven on earth, to be encouraged in your faith in the middle of every day. God just may have something big to show you in a humble person on the corner.

And to those of you feeling hopeful, waiting on your bus: let me remind you that God always shows up on time. He's working it out right now. He's moving mountains and making a better way. While you wait on a bus, He's preparing to deliver you a friend to encourage you to keep pressing on and believing in miracles, like my sweet friend that I met on the street corner that day. Don't think for one second that you've been forgotten. He sees you on that corner. A bus, a miracle, a friend is on its way.

RESPONSE:

Has an interruption in your life ever been an opening for God to work for good for your sake or that of someone else?

_____

_____

_____

_____

_____

_____

_____

_____

PRAYER:

_____

_____

_____

_____

_____

_____

_____

_____

_____

Be still, and know that I am God. I will be exalted among the nations, I will be exalted in the earth!

PSALM 46:10

day 26

I will be exalted in the earth!

PSALM 46:10

Have you ever overslept? I don't mean hit the snooze button kind of oversleeping, but the completely miss your alarm and wake up two hours late kind of oversleeping. This happened to me not too long ago, and I remember the rush of panic that instantly flooded my heart when I opened my eyes and looked at the time. I almost leaped out of bed, but something in me was challenged to embrace it and enjoy it. So I stayed in bed for a moment longer, enjoying the peace of morning, letting my to-do list stay in the "pending" drawer just a bit longer. I didn't say anything, but it was the most prayerful and still moment I had allowed myself in awhile. The night before, I'd had terrible stomach pain. It hurt so bad that I was curled up in the fetal position. I needed medicine but standing up and driving to the pharmacy was not physically possible. I was laid out on my back, forced into stillness. Then, I was reminded of the beauty of selflessness and humbled beyond belief when my best friend offered to pick up the medicine I needed and bring me some tea. Not only that but as the pain seemed to get worse, she gently rubbed my back until I fell into a deep slumber. The gentleness in her heart and her willingness to put aside her own schedule taught me something.

This is how I am created to be: to sit at the feet of Jesus, learn gentleness, peace, and selflessness, and then give it away. Give it all away, like my friend did that night. But I won't have anything to give away if I don't enjoy His peace, put off my schedule and to-do list, and let His peace lay me flat on my back. Stillness is necessary for our souls, and peace is a big deal. Peace with God is a gift and peace with people is a call —a call to love gently and give freely. Let's depend on Jesus and live like that today.

Be still
and know
that I
am God

PSALM 46:10

For what does it profit a man to gain the whole world and forfeit his soul?

MARK 8:36

day 27

For what does it profit a man to gain the whole world and forfeit his soul?

MARK 8:36

Some mornings I wake up with hundreds of hurried thoughts rattling around in my brain, and they often sound something like this:

Already out of coffee? I'll stop at Starbucks.
Laundry is way overdue. Need to get to that today.
Oh gosh, I need to grocery shop, too.
Does my hair really have to be so difficult today?
Can I squeeze in a quick devotional? Shoot, I'm already 10 minutes behind.
I need to be more like *insert name here.*
I should probably try to make more money.
And I need to call that wedding vendor today.
Oh shoot, I forgot to email her back.
Oh, meeting at 3. Can't forget.
Man, I need to work out at some point today.
This outfit makes me look weird.
I'm way behind on that project.
How am I going to get everything done?

Chasing after this world makes me tired. Exhausted, really. I run, I worry, I push, shove, kick, and fight to squeeze everything into every sacred moment. I look around and ask how I can achieve more, do more, profit more, and be more. This world makes some snazzy advertisements, tempting me to work for its promises, submit to its demands, to sell my soul. But what profit will that bring me? Nothing.

To those of you worrying if you're doing enough, being enough, achieving enough, and to those of you feeling overwhelmed and overdone, let this be an encouragement to you: the value of our souls doesn't work like a vending machine. By that, I mean that it doesn't increase or decrease based on the amount of stuff we do or don't do. Our souls are worthy and valuable because of Jesus. And you're invited to tune out the shouts of this world, the distractions of the day, and be okay right where you are.

RESPONSE:

Where do you find rest in your day? Describe what it would look like to rest in Jesus.

_____

_____

_____

_____

_____

_____

_____

PRAYER:

_____

_____

_____

_____

_____

_____

_____

At that time Jesus declared, "I thank you, Father, Lord of heaven and earth, that you have hidden these things from the wise and understanding and revealed them to little children; yes, Father, for such was your gracious will. All things have been handed over to me by my Father, and no one knows the Son except the Father, and no one knows the Father except the Son and anyone to whom the Son chooses to reveal him. Come to me, all who labor and are heavy laden, and I will give you rest. Take my yoke upon you, and learn from me, for I am gentle and lowly in heart, and you will find rest for your souls. For my yoke is easy, and my burden is light."

MATTHEW 11:25-30

day 28

"Come to me...and I will give you rest."

MATTHEW 11:28

This past holiday season, I went to a sporting goods store to pick up some dumbbells for my brother for Christmas. I hadn't thought about how my weak little arms would lift 60-pound weights. So, being the graceful gal that I am, I made all the weights tumble onto the floor as soon as I tried to lug one from the rack into my cart. Needless to say, I caused quite the scene. I wanted to crawl into a hole and hide with comfort food and Christmas carols. Thankfully, a man rushed to my aid. And I was reminded of the beauty of a helper. My pride tells me I can carry the weight on my own. But my weaknesses inevitably prevail as I'm left standing in the middle of the mess with all the heaviness hitting the floor. And I realize that I desperately need a helping hand, a friend, and a Savior.

Maybe that's you, too. Sometimes the weight of the world can get really, really heavy. So if you're feeling the weight of the world on your shoulders, or just a load that's a few pounds too heavy to carry on your own, that's okay. You don't have to be strong all the time. We all have burdens that are slightly too heavy and crosses that are hard to carry alone. But there's good news. We can look up to see with our eyes and believe in our hearts that we have a helper and a friend in Jesus. A savior who comes to our aid, bears our burdens and lightens our load as He places our cross on His own shoulders when life gets just a little bit too heavy. His yoke is easy and His burden is light.

So drop the weight, sweet friend. You weren't made to carry it alone.

for my
yoke is
easy and
my burden
is light

MATT 11:30

For Macedonia and Achaia have been
pleased to make some contribution for the
poor among the saints at Jerusalem. For they
were pleased to do it, and indeed they owe
it to them. For if the Gentiles have come to
share in their spiritual blessings, they ought
also to be of service to them in material
blessings. When therefore I have completed
this and have delivered to them what has
been collected, I will leave for Spain by way
of you. I know that when I come to you I will
come in the fullness of the blessing of Christ.

ROMANS 15:26-29

day 29

For they were pleased to do it...

ROMANS 15:27

A few weeks ago at church, the pastor made the "be a good steward with your resources" sermon. You know the one I'm talking about. The one that makes you want to disappear in your seat and poof out of existence as they pass the plate around. Giving is meant to be joyful but it can be so painful. Especially when things are tight. I wanted to tune out the pastor's words and hold on to the change in my purse.

As I sat there, something struck me as we dove into Romans 15. The gospel gives us the freedom of an open-handed life—much like Macedonia and Achaia's willingness to give joyfully to the poor, as if it were owed, despite their own desperate state of need. This passage uses the language of debt, reminding us of our spiritual responsibility to participate in the mission of God. To give largely and liberally, not grudgingly, requires a new heart because we often curl our fingers around our money, time, and future. We are wrong, and our motives are often wrong, but Jesus connects the gospel and generosity.

Perhaps money has been tight and giving just doesn't seem in the cards for you this week, month, or year. Let this be an encouragement that there is both joy and responsibility in giving. Joy is part of giving because God is a cheerful giver and we are invited to join in the mission of God. Responsibility is a part of giving because our resources are really not our own but instead, that of the Giver. We need help to hold our own plans, time, resources, and lives loosely. Thank God for His gospel, which constantly creates a generous life yielded to God when we open our hands and accept the invitation to participate in His mission (Vroegop, 2015).

RESPONSE:

How can you practice generosity today?

_____
_____
_____
_____
_____
_____
_____
_____
_____
_____
_____
_____

PRAYER:

_____
_____
_____
_____
_____
_____
_____
_____
_____
_____
_____
_____
_____

But he said to me, "My grace is sufficient for you, for my power is made perfect in weakness."

Therefore I will boast all the more gladly of my weaknesses, so that the power of Christ may rest upon me. For the sake of Christ, then, I am content with weaknesses, insults, hardships, persecutions, and calamities. For when I am weak, then I am strong.

2 CORINTHIANS 12:9-10

day 30

For when I am weak, then I am strong.

2 CORINTHIANS 12:10

Every day I wake up messy. My hair is disheveled, I have dragon breath, and my eyes are puffy with sleep. I have to stand in front of a mirror, splash water on my face, brush the gunk from my teeth, and throw on some makeup before I present myself to the world outside. Most mornings, I've already spent my first hour of the day worrying about what I'll wear, accomplish, do, and be that day, knowing it'll never be enough and probably won't be all that graceful. I struggle to get it all together. It takes time and energy just to make my outside look put together. And it takes Jesus to clean up the messiness of my heart.

To those of you feeling unattractive, uncoordinated, or unworthy, do you want to hear something awesome?

I don't have to fake it or pretend that I have it all together. And neither do you. Contrary to popular belief, in Christ we are invited to expose our mess, knowing that He gives us His light in its place. We don't have to pretend we have it all together all the time because life isn't meant to be perfect. It's messy and needy. If it weren't, there would be no need for Jesus. Our imperfections are not flaws, but opportunities to see God's glory. And that's what a life in Jesus looks like: filters off and freedom found.

Freedom from the chains of this earth. Freedom from the power of death.

So don't forget that in the middle of your mess, His grace is sufficient for you, too.

my
grace
is
sufficient
for you

2 COR. 12:9

And the master said to the servant, "Go out to the highways and hedges and compel people to come in, that my house may be filled. For I tell you, none of those men who were invited shall taste my banquet."

LUKE 14:23-24

day 31

"Go out...and compel people to come in..."

LUKE 14:23

Sometimes I feel awfully lonely. I begin to wonder if I really belong and whether people would notice if I were gone. It's a result of a longing to feel relevant, accepted, and loved. A few weeks ago, as I was wallowing in my sorrows, I struck up a conversation with a young woman at a bus stop. It turned out that she was from China, working on her graduate degree. She shared her story with me: how she came to the United States two years ago, leaving her family and friends behind. Somewhere along the line she mentioned that she was used to being alone most of the time. My heart ached as I realized how similar we were—we both longed for that feeling of love and acceptance, despite the difference in our cultural experiences. My encounter with her reminded me to stop asking, "how can I belong?" and instead ask, "how can I make others belong?"

So if you're wondering if you belong, if there's a place for you at the table, the answer is yes. You have a place at the greatest feast when you accept Jesus' invitation. There's a place set for you. But there's also a place set for your guest. Bring someone along. Instead of worrying if you belong, I challenge you to reach out in a way you wouldn't normally. Be the church. Say hello to the girl at the bus stop. And invite her to the feast where everyone belongs. Her heart longs for Jesus' love as much as yours does.

RESPONSE:

How can you help others find a sense of belonging?

_____
_____
_____
_____
_____
_____
_____
_____
_____
_____
_____
_____
_____

PRAYER:

_____
_____
_____
_____
_____
_____
_____
_____
_____
_____
_____
_____

"Therefore I tell you, do not be anxious
about your life, what you will eat or what
you will drink, nor about your body, what
you will put on. Is not life more than food,
and the body more than clothing?..But
seek first the kingdom of God and his
righteousness, and all these things will
be added to you."

MATTHEW 6:25-34

day 32

Consider the lilies of the field...

MATTHEW 6:28

Here's a riddle: Which comes first, the supply or the need?

The first time I heard this riddle I quickly answered, "The need!" Any economist will tell you that, logically, a certain need leads to a supply. If people need food, they farm and grow a supply of vegetables to last through the winter. If people need clean water, a water filter company emerges and profits. If people need clothing, they sew and stitch until the supply is enough to meet the need. But the old man who posed the question to me smiled softly as he said, "Yes, perhaps. But in God's kingdom, the supply is always there before the need. Just in time, every time."

So if you're in desperate need, running low on faith, remember that He gives us enough before we even know we need it. He's already got us taken care of, provided for, and protected before the hour comes that we recognize we need it. And when we do realize our need, the supply will always be delivered before it's too late. Every single time.

consider
the lilies
of the field...
MATT 6:28

NOTES:

NOTES:

NOTES:

NOTES:

ABOUT THE AUTHOR

jordan lee

First and foremost, I belong to Jesus Christ, and I'm passionate about encouraging friends like you in Truth. My favorite verse is Psalm 37:4 — it's a reminder to seek the Lord in all that I do and to delight in Him so that He can mold and shape the desires of my heart.

I'm from the Midwest, an Indiana girl born and raised. Indiana is known for having a whole lot of cornfields. They are fields of gold and little reminders of simple beauty that I've grown to really love! I feel God most when I'm in His Word and in His world, enjoying the beauty of His creation out in nature. He is so big and so alive! I hope that studying the Word creatively will help make that feeling a reality for you, too!

www.thesoulscripts.com | @soulscripts

REFERENCES:

Donehey, Mike. (2010, April 26). Tenth Avenue North. Retrieved January, 2016, from https://www.youtube.com/watch?v=7CO6ycaEY6A&feature=youtu.be

Keller, Tim. (2012). *The Freedom of Self Forgetfulness: The Path to the True Christian Joy.* Leyland: 10Publishing.

Hughes, Barbara. (2013). *Disciplines of a Godly Woman.* Wheaton, IL: Crossway Books.

To Know Christ and to Make Him Known® - The Navigators. Retrieved January, 2016, from http://www.navigators.org/Home

Stone, Diana. (2014, November 30). *Give Thanks in Wandering.* Retrieved January, 2016, from http://shereadstruth.com/2014/11/27/give-thanks-wandering/

Vroegop, Mark. (2015, November 8). *The Gospel Creates Generosity.* Retrieved January, 2016, from http://www.yourchurch.com/sermon/the-gospel-creates-generosity/